The power of forgiveness

Contact address: Oteng Montshiti
P O Box M680
Kanye
Botswana

E-mail address: otengmontshiti@gmail.com
Contact number: (+267) 74 644 954

Acknowledgements

Writing a book is a challenging task which requires time. I would like thank my family especially my lovely wife for supporting me.

Table of contents

Introduction

Deuteronomy 30:19 I call heaven and earth to record this day against you, *that* I have set before you life and death, blessing and cursing: therefore choose life, that both thou and thy seed may live:

Deuteronomy 30:20 That thou mayest love the LORD thy God, *and* that thou mayest obey his voice, and that thou mayest cleave unto him: for he *is* thy life, and the length of thy days: that thou mayest dwell in the land which the LORD sware unto thy fathers, to Abraham, to Isaac, and to Jacob, to give them.

Life is full of choices and one day you are going to face the consequences of your actions. In this world, if you choose to reject the ways of the Lord you will reap what you have sown. You will reap pain. But if you choose the ways of the Lord, you will reap joy, a life of abundance and fulfillment. Do you know why? Because God didn't create you as a robotic being. No matter what happens, the Lord won't override your will.

As a human being, you consist of three major components, body, soul and spirit. Your body is the outer shell you use to interact with the outside world. For example, you use your hands to receive blessings like money, cars, and much more. Spirit is the real you.

When God speaks to you, He speaks to your spirit. The moment you are born again, your spirit is regenerated. Your spirit doesn’t sleep when you fall asleep. It is always active. That's why you always dream about certain events or things because God uses your spirit to communicate with you. That's to say, the type of friends you must keep, the decision you should make in life, and much more.

Then, there is the soul, which is a sit of intelligence, emotions, and willpower. Willpower is where you make your decisions. Do you know why? Because the Lord acts out of infinitive love, He doesn't impose his will on people. Even in the beginning in heaven, the angelic were created with the power of choice. The fallen angels rebelled against God out of their will. They were exercising it when they joined hands with the devil and tried to overthrow the legitimate government of God and failed. Then, they were cast out of the presence of the Lord. Life is full of choices, indeed.

For instance, Jesus Christ obeyed the Lord's instructions to the letter like forgiving his persecutors out of godly love. He healed the sick and so forth out of compassion. He did the will of his father on earth out of his undying love for God.

Therefore, forgiving other people is a choice. Meaning you aren't forced to do it. If you decide to walk down the path of forgiveness and reconciliation, unlimited benefits are awaiting you at the end of the tunnel. So, you must forgive everybody who has wronged you, even your worst enemy.

Chapter 1

What is forgiveness?

Mark 11:25 And when ye stand praying, forgive, if ye have ought against any: that your Father also which is in heaven may forgive you your trespasses.

Mark 11:26 But if ye do not forgive, neither will your Father which is in heaven forgive your trespasses.

Forgiveness is a personal decision to let go of offenses and choose the path of reconciliation. It is one of the spiritual gifts from the throne of God. Remember, a gift can be rejected or accepted. It is upon the recipient. God has given you the gift of forgiveness. You must receive it for your personal benefits.

Therefore, as a human being, you must learn to forgive and forget because forgiveness is the vehicle that you use to reach a life of prosperity, inner peace, and success.

Chapter 2

Forgiveness is a sign of strength

Many people under the sun have a misconception about the issue of forgiveness. They view it as a sign of weakness. Because of this husbands can't gather their spouses around the table and apologize for their bad behavior. They can't ask forgiveness from their children. Do you know why? Because they think that their partner and children are lesser than them. Just because the bible says, the husband is the head of the family. Now, they think that if they apologize, they will be weakening themselves.

If you lack forgiveness, you will be consumed within. As time goes by, you will become a shell of your former self. Lack of forgiveness is a poisonous material that kills your potential and strength. When it has fully eaten you within, you will develop lots of sicknesses like distress, and much more. When you forgive others, you offload that luggage that is weighing you down

and you regain your strength. One day, a certain brother had a conflict with one of his siblings. He vowed he would never forgive her. Then, his life deteriorated and ultimately crumble into a heap of shame. Guess what happened?

One day he met one of his friends who was a covenant child of the Lord and narrated the whole incident to him.

Then, he threw the most challenging question to him, "have you forgiven your sister?" and said, "No." Thereafter, he told him the root cause of his problem and asked him to approach his sister and iron out their differences. He obeyed his words and guess what happened? His life was restored. He felt like a bag of cement had been lifted off his shoulder.

Chapter 3

The power of forgiveness

It has the power to heal

A certain young lady approached a particular psychologist who was a child of the living God. She told her he was distressed because her younger sister had used her savings without her permission. He went on and said, she twist at night because of that. Then, the psychologist asked to go and tell God sincerely what she had told her in her secret room of prayer. She went home and did exactly that.

Her first attempt seemed to be futile and as she pressed on, she felt an icy sensation in her heart.

Then, she told her the following day to approach her sister again and iron out their differences. Wasting no time she rushed to her house and apologized to her for holding grudges against her. They embraced one another and promised to pay her in installments. They agreed. Since that day the pain which had twirling in her heart was eradicated and inner peace reigned in her heart. She started to sleep peacefully like a baby. That's the power of forgiveness in action. It has the power to heal the broken-hearted.

If you decide to walk down the path of lack of forgiveness, you are simply venturing into a suicide mission. Because you will be consumed on the inside. When you are depressed, you can't sleep peacefully at night. But God has promised his beloved sweet sleep. So, don't embrace the life of self-destruction. Remember, you are the only person who has the solution to your problems, and forgiveness is the only path to your salvation.

Therefore, you must cultivate a habit of letting go of offenses to be healed. If you are wounded on the inside, forgiveness is the master key to a life of peace and abundance.

It has the power to restore broken homes

Statistical information reveals that divorce rates are on the rise. Marriages are under constant attack from the kingdom of the dark side. The courts are overwhelmed. The society that we live in has slid into a deplorable state of despair, as the basic unit of the community is dismantled. But there is hope. It is found within the pages of the Holy Scriptures. It is found within the realm of forgiveness and reconciliation.

As human beings, we mustn't allow fleshly desires to dominate us. Remember, if homes are broken automatically, the future of nations looks dull. It is an issue of concern that must be addressed urgently. For example, it is sickening to the stomach to hear seventieth-something couples heading for divorce because of irreconcilable differences. It is stunning because the elderly people must guide the youth in the right ways of the Lord.

God has provided you with the way out of your predicament as a family. Don't allow the devil to use you by holding grudges against other people. Just forgive and forget. You must forgive your partner. Instead of running to the high court and filing for divorce, seek reconciliation. That's what the Lord wants.

Today, children are unpleasantly labelling their parents. They are calling them many names like witches, wizards, and so on because somebody told them so. Do you know why? Because a traditional doctor has thrown bones on the ground and spoke words that don't build. Instead of building, they have planted seeds of hatred among family members.

If you have been calling your parents such names, you are destroying their dignity and reputation. So, just swallow your pride before it is too late and apologize to them. I can assure you God is on the throne. He will restore what your family has lost. Meaning that he will restore the peace, harmony, and joy you used to enjoy as a family. Just imagine having a meaningful conversation, cracking jokes, and so forth as a unit. You know, empowering one another. Indeed, forgiveness is the most integral part of your existence as a human being.

If the devil destroys families automatically, your nation is going to be in danger. Because it is the place where young children are brought up by elderly people to fit perfectly in society. This process is known as socialization. Now, if the foundation has been destroyed, the structure is going to crumble into a heap of disgrace. Because it is going to give birth to a nation that doesn't embrace and recognize the value of forgiveness. Therefore, if at the family level children are taught the value of forgiveness and reconciliation, they will attain unlimited glory. It is the sincere desire of the Lord for family members to forgive one another. By so doing, they are going what the Lord wants before the foundations of the world.

It has the power to restore friendship

In this world friendship without forgiveness won't stand the test of time. True friendship is whereby two different people establish a brotherly or sisterly covenant. One day a certain brother stormed into my house, fuming. I told him to calm down after offering him a cold cup of water. After he had sipped, and cold down I asked him his problem. He told me that one of his friends had wrecked his car after borrowing it.

He further said his friend like to travel at sickening speed. Thereafter, I told him to his face that he ignored the red flags by going ahead and gave him the car knowing that he was a careless driver. Therefore, he should have used wisdom and not gave him the car. Because he was going to preserve their friendship.

As friends, he should have identify his weakness and come up with a way to overcome them. After hearing that he shot to his feet and approached his friend who agreed to repair the wrecked car. From there he stopped what he had been doing and continued as friends even up to today. You see, how the power of the spirit of forgiveness works.

According to the bible, after the fall of man in the Garden of Eden God out of infinite love sat a r edemptive plan into motion because sin had turned man into God's enemy. Remember, seasons change but the nature of the Lord abides forever. He hates sin but loves sinners. Centuries passed the messiah was nowhere to be found. At the right time, Jesus Christ was born, raised, and died for your sins. Today, when you are born again you are longer called an enemy of the Lord but his friend. In other words, with the blood of Jesus Christ that was shed on the cross of Calvary, God has forgiven people of their sins through it.

Chapter 4

Forgive those who persecute you

Matthew 5:44 But I say unto you, Love your enemies, bless them that curse you, do good to them that hate you, and pray for them which despitefully use you, and persecute you;

Under the sun it is easy to curse people who persecute you but it is hard to bless them. As you all know that life is full of choices, you can choose the path of blessings or curses. It is all up to you. But one thing is certain it is human nature to revenge by using ungodly words which release curses over the lives of others. As a covenant child of the living God, you must learn to forgive and forget. Otherwise, you won't make it in life. Do you know that Jesus Christ blessed his enemies when he was hanging on the cross? Yes, he did. Because he knew that if you don't forgive those who persecute you, you will be like them before the Lord, to make matters worse, it hinders your breakthrough.

When he was hanging on the cross he said, "Father forgive them because they don't know what they are going." Remember, he is your roadmap and you must imitate him. You are called to reveal the nature of the Lord on earth so that other people can know him and come to him through that.

Chapter 5

If you don’t forgive other people God won’t

Matthew 5:44 But I say unto you, Love your enemies, bless them that curse you, do good to them that hate you, and pray for them which despitefully use you, and persecute you;

Matthew 5:45 That ye may be the children of your Father which is in heaven: for he maketh his sun to rise on the evil and on the good, and sendeth rain on the just and on the unjust.

One day, Jesus Christ's followers gathered around him and asked the Lord to teach them how to pray. He didn't beat around the bush and said, "….forgive us our trespasses as we forgive those who wronged us." this clearly shows that you must ask forgiveness from the Lord and forgive other people. If you don't forgive your fellow brethren God automatically won't forgive you. It is a spiritual principle that many people aren't aware of. This means if you don't forgive them you must forget about heaven. Yes, do you know that if you embrace the spirit of lack of forgiveness you won't inherit the kingdom of God?

You can't live in the presence of the Lord when your heart is saturated with the spirit of lack of forgiveness. It is highly impossible because it is sin before God. You can't stand before him putting on the nature of the devil. No matter how much you justify your actions. You see, how deadly a lack of forgiveness is? You will be cast out of the presence of the living God to where there is gnashing of teeth. You will be there at the mercy of the father of all lies the devil in the everlasting flames of hell. Remember, there is no forgiveness of sin beyond the grave. So, do the right thing while you are still alive and let go of offenses.

Chapter 6

Forgiveness is the nature of God

Psalm 86:5 For thou, Lord, *art* good, and ready to forgive; and plenteous in mercy unto all them that call upon thee.

There are two spiritual fathers namely the devil and God. When you aren't born again you carry the nature of the devil. In other words, he is your spiritual father. The nature of the devil is the desire of the flesh like lack of forgiveness, bitterness, and revenge. These are the deadly weapons the devil uses to destroy humanity. If you embrace them you are destined to be eternally destroyed by God unless you repent. While the nature of the Lord is the opposite of the devil's such as forgiveness, love, peace, and much more. If you have them you are demonstrating to the entire world that you are a follower of Jesus Christ and he is your spiritual father.

As a covenant child of the Lord, you must embrace his nature because as he is in heaven so are we in the world. In other words, you are called to reveal his glory on earth. When you forgive and forget your character on its own is going to win souls for the Lord. Because the greatest evangelism is when you treat other people the way God would have treated them.

Chapter 7

How many times should you forgive other people?

Luke 17:3 Take heed to yourselves: If thy brother trespass against thee, rebuke him; and if he repent, forgive him.

Luke 17:4 And if he trespass against thee seven times in a day, and seven times in a day turn again to thee, saying, I repent; thou shalt forgive him.

One day Peter asked Jesus Christ how many times he must forgive his fellow brethren. Jesus Christ as the revelation of the Lord on earth didn't beat about the bush he told him that he must do that seven times in the day. In other words, he should forgive them countless times. You must imitate the Lord because if He were to count our sins none of us would escape his wrath or judgment.

So, as a covenant child of the lord, you must do the right thing forgive and forget. It isn't a once-of thing it is a lifelong process. You should practice it as long as you are breathing under the sun. Because Jesus Christ your roadmap forgave those who persecuted him throughout his lifetime. He even forgave those who crucified him. That's a clear example that you must forgive and forget throughout your lifetime. Because lack of forgiveness kills your creativity until you crawl to your grave. Remember, the fear of death is nothing compared to dying without Jesus Christ because you will be tormented day and night in the bottomless pit.

Chapter 8

Steps of forgiveness

Everybody has sinned and needs forgiveness from God

Romans 3:23 For all have sinned, and come short of the glory of God;

Everybody under the sun has sinned against the Lord and sincerely needs forgiveness. If you think you are smart and you don't need it, well you are wrong. That is known as self-deception. So, don't deceive yourself. After the fall of Adam and Eve sin entered the entire world. The nature of the devil-like lack of forgiveness started to dominate human beings. Instead of embracing forgiveness, peace love, harmony joy, and much more became distant memories.

Centuries went by, and still, the situation remained the same. Until Jesus Christ stepped on the scene and died on the cross in your place (as a substitution). Today, you must realize that you need his forgiveness the more. Then, you can look around you and identify people you have wounded and release them from your heart. In simple words, you must realize that God didn't reject you when you ask him to forgive you all your sins. Similarly, you must realize that you have been forgiven to forgive others.

Obey the infallible word of the Lord

Deuteronomy 28:1 And it shall come to pass, if thou shalt hearken diligently unto the voice of the LORD thy God, to observe *and* to do all his commandments which I command thee this day, that the LORD thy God will set thee on high above all nations of the earth:

The word of God is a treasure that needs to be discovered. It is a spiritual mystery that needs the right spiritual tools to decode it to be empowered and successful in life. Yes, to be successful because forgiveness is a success on its own. Under the sun or heaven, I have never seen a person who lacks forgiveness make it in life.

The word of God is a spiritual item and forgiveness is spiritual. It is a tool that you use as a covenant child of the Lord to fling doors of breakthrough wide open. So, if you make the word of the living God integral part of your being I can assure you that heaven is your limit.

It isn't by human power but by the spirit of God

Zechariah 4:6 Then he answered and spake unto me, saying, This *is* the word of the LORD unto Zerubbabel, saying, Not by might, nor by power, but by my spirit, saith the LORD of hosts.

Human strength has its weaknesses and strength. But to forgive and forget you can't use it. In other words, it takes God's grace to do that. People on their own they like revenge. When you have wounded them it's their nature to repay one other with evil. However, one great person once said, an eye for an eye makes the world go blind. It is true because they are wars, tribal hatred, bitterness, uncontrollable anger, and so on everywhere. Evil has enveloped the hearts of people.

To forgive and forget you need the spirit of God to do that. Without it, you will always fly into a rage when you see people who have wrong you. But with the aid of the Holy Spirit, you forgive and forget

The end

www.ingramcontent.com/pod-product-compliance
Ingram Content Group UK Ltd.
Pitfield, Milton Keynes, MK11 3LW, UK
UKHW021644190726
13853UKWH00001B/39